Franklin D. Roosevelt's Inaugural Address of 1933

Introduction by
Raymond H. Geselbracht

MILESTONE DOCUMENTS IN THE NATIONAL ARCHIVES

National Archives and Records Administration

Washington, DC

Published for the
National Archives and Records Administration
By the National Archives Trust Fund Board
1988

Library of Congress Cataloging-in-Publication Data

Roosevelt, Franklin D. (Franklin Delano), 1882-1945.
    Franklin D. Roosevelt's inaugural address of 1933.

    (Milestone documents in the National Archives)
    Bibliography: p.
    1. United States — Politics and government — 1933-1945.
2. Presidents — United States — Inaugural addresses —
Facsimiles. I. United States. National Archives and
Records Administration. II. Title. III. Series.
E742.5.R65   1988   973.917'092'4   88-600066
ISBN 0-911333-69-X

An Introduction

Franklin D. Roosevelt came to the Presidency in the midst of the greatest economic chaos the nation has ever known. Three-and-a-half years of deterioration had passed since the stock market crash of October and November 1929: industrial output had dropped by March 1933 to half its 1929 level; nearly 15 million people were unemployed, about one-fourth of the labor force; business bankruptcies and farm mortgage foreclosures were widespread; the banking system was on the verge of collapse. Homeless and hungry people lived in shacks made of rubbish and scavenged for food like wild animals. Outbreaks of violence indicated the determination of some Americans to fight against the economic system which was taking everything they had away from them. For the first time, in the election of 1932, the Communist Party openly announced itself and ran a candidate for president. Some people spoke of the possibility of an open revolution.

The nation had suffered through a 4-month interregnum period since Roosevelt's election in November, during which time the economic crisis steadily deepened and the mood of the country became increasingly desperate. Lame-duck President Herbert Hoover's own personal mood had grown darkly incommunicative. He had failed, and he had been rejected by the American people at the polls. His attitude to the President-elect was made clear in one of his campaign speeches. If Roosevelt should come to power, he warned, "the grass will grow in the streets of a hundred cities, a thousand towns; the weeds will overrun the fields of millions of farms." Roosevelt, in contrast to the gloomy Hoover, felt hopeful about the country's future and was eager to begin work on solving its problems. He had promised, in one of his campaign speeches, to bring a "new deal" to the American people. His other campaign speeches had given clues as to what this "new deal" was to be, but he was depending upon his inaugural address to give a clear statement of the aspirations of his Presidency. On March 2, 1933, Roosevelt took the train from New York to Washington, DC, carrying with him the speech he would deliver in 2 days.

A considerable mystery surrounds the drafting of Roosevelt's first inaugural address. It is not entirely clear who did the writing: did the President-elect work alone, or nearly so, or did he merely reshape someone else's work? The evidence is confusing. According to Rexford Tugwell, one of the five men referred to collectively during the 1932 campaign as the "Brain Trust," Roosevelt had no artistic sense and no literary feeling; he could pen a good line now and again, usually giving a biblical lilt to his words, but he was not a good speech writer. Roosevelt sought to achieve in his speeches something of Woodrow Wilson's eloquence and Theodore Roosevelt's vividness and vigor, but he relied on others to prepare drafts for him, which he would then alter.

Despite Roosevelt's preference for having others draft his speeches, the most frequently repeated view of the drafting of the first inaugural address is that Roosevelt wrote it himself, unaided, sitting by his fireside in his library at Hyde Park, New York, in the late night and early morning of February 27 and 28, 1933. This rather romantic view was first put forward by Samuel I. Rosenman, another Brain Trust member, in his book *Working with Roosevelt* (1952) and is included in a widely-read early biography of Roosevelt, James MacGregor Burns' *Roosevelt: The Lion and the Fox* (1956). Rosenman, who was not with the President-elect during his night of speech writing, presents as evidence for his view a draft of the address in Roosevelt's handwriting and an attached, typed note, dated March 25, 1933, in which Roosevelt seems to claim sole authorship. "I started it about 9:00 p.m. and ended at 1:30 a.m.," the note says. "A number of minor changes were made in subsequent drafts but the final draft is substantially the same as this original." The most important change was the addition of the famous phrase "the only thing we have to fear is fear itself," which is not present in the handwritten draft. According to Rosenman's account, which is admittedly circumstantial, Roosevelt must have added the "fear" phrase after he arrived in Washington, on March 2d or 3d. The inspiration for the addition was assumed to be Henry David Thoreau's line, "Nothing is so much to be feared as fear." Mrs. Roosevelt told Rosenman that her husband had a copy of some of Thoreau's writings in his hotel suite.

A very different view of the writing of the first inaugural address was put forward in 1966 by another member of the Brain Trust, Raymond Moley, who presents his evidence in his book *The First New Deal* (1966). Work on the inaugural address began, he says, on the night of September 22, 1932, almost 6 weeks before the election. Moley had met with Roosevelt for 3 hours, discussing the speech in terms of the national emergency and consequent need for strong Presidential authority. Moley took no notes at the meeting, for fear they might somehow reach the Republican opposition, which, he felt, would certainly accuse Roosevelt of being an aspiring dictator.

Unemployed men queued outside a Depression soup kitchen that was opened in Chicago by gangster Al Capone, February 1931. (306-NT-165.319c, National Archives)

First "New Deal" Cartoon!

Upon request we are reprinting the first cartoon of the New Deal. It was drawn by our cartoonist, John Baer, on January 1, 1931. It appeared in hundreds of newspapers at the time and it was credited as an inspiration for the New Deal phrase on which the late Franklin D. Roosevelt rode to victory. When Governor of New York state, he acknowledged a letter in which Baer sent a copy of the cartoon and said, "You know how deeply I appreciate all that you are doing to shape public opinion through your cartoons and news letter." Recently a member of the Roosevelt Cabinet stated that the phrase, New Deal, had originated from John Baer's cartoon. Mr. Roosevelt made his first reference to a New Deal on July 2, 1932, in Chicago, when he said in accepting the Democratic nomination for the presidency, "I pledge myself to a New Deal to the American people." John thinks that while organized labor had a great victory in the last elections there is nevertheless a coalition of reactionary Republicans and Bourbon Democrats which still controls both houses of Congress. In 1956, we shall need a New Deck as well as a New Deal, and workers have the balance of power which will swing it.

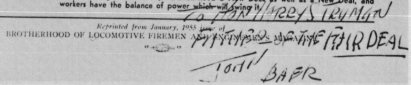

Reprinted from January, 1955 issue of
BROTHERHOOD OF LOCOMOTIVE FIREMEN AND ENGINEMEN'S MAGAZINE

Political cartoonist John Baer drew the above sketch January 1, 1931 — in the middle of Hoover's Administration. It appeared in hundreds of newspapers and caught Roosevelt's attention for he understood that this cartoon had captured the sense of most Americans concerning their plight. FDR's "New Deal" promised programs for relief, recovery, and reform — a platform that easily carried him to victory at the polls. (72-325, Harry S. Truman Library)

Moley reports that he next met with Roosevelt to discuss the inaugural address on the night of February 3, 1933. This time notes were taken, both by Moley and by another of Roosevelt's aides. The next morning Moley converted the notes into 12 pages of ideas for the inaugural address. On February 12 and 13, he prepared a draft from these notes. His secretary typed it, and Moley destroyed the handwritten draft, again to protect against the opposition prematurely learning the tenor of the inaugural address. From time to time during the next 2 weeks, Moley tinkered with his draft; toward the end of the month he prepared a revised version, which he carried with him to Hyde Park for the long night's work of speechwriting with Roosevelt on February 27-28.

According to Moley, Roosevelt and Moley began work in the library at about nine o'clock. Roosevelt read over Moley's draft, then borrowed his yellow legal pad to do the work of revision in his own hand so that his long-time aide, Louis Howe, would not, as Roosevelt said, "have a fit." (Presumably the fierce Howe wanted the President-elect to write his own speech.) Roosevelt sat with a folding table in front of him, writing; Moley sat on a sofa in front of the fireplace. Every sentence of the draft was read aloud and considered by the two men. Sometimes one, sometimes the other, would suggest a change, and Roosevelt would scribble down the result. As the hours went by, Moley became more and more aware of the importance of the homey speechwriting session of which he was privileged to be a part. At 11 p.m. he wrote a few words in his notebook: "A week — yes five days — this man will be Pres. of U.S. . . . A strong man F.D.R." The speech they were preparing was not simply words; it expressed the ideas that would soon guide the policies and make the laws of the United States Government. Moley was moved. When the speechwriting work was completed and Roosevelt's handwritten draft lay on the table in front of him, Moley rose from the sofa, took his typed draft up from the table and threw it into the fire. "This is your speech now," he told the President-elect.

Typical outdoor soup kitchen during the Depression era, New York 1932. (306-NT-172-081c, National Archives)

The next morning, Moley continues, he went over Roosevelt's handwritten draft, making a few changes. The draft as he left it, in Roosevelt's hand and with Moley's few scribbled changes, is preserved in the President's speech file at the Franklin D. Roosevelt Library in Hyde Park; and Roosevelt's note, seemingly claiming sole authorship, is attached. According to Moley, the "nothing to fear" phrase was added on the morning of February 28 by Louis Howe, who probably got it, not from Thoreau's writings, but from a considerably more humble source — a department store's newspaper advertisement. Next to the handwritten draft in

Unemployed bachelor, abandoned mining camp of Jere, Pennsylvania, March 1937. He spoke English poorly but indicated that he was grateful to the federal government by displaying a picture of the President on the wall. (69-RP-8-113, National Archives)

the speech file is a typed draft containing the "fear" phrase and dated March 1, 1933, the day before the President-elect left Hyde Park for Washington.

On March 3, the day before the inauguration, Moley writes that he and Roosevelt went over the draft of the inaugural address. They made a few minor changes and then gave the draft to a typist to prepare a reading copy. When the typing was finished, Moley put the speech in his coat pocket, and that night he put it under his pillow, still guarding his and Roosevelt's precious work from premature disclosure. The next morning, inauguration day, he gave the speech to the President-elect.

This is the end of Moley's account of the drafting of the first inaugural address. He did not, he insists, discover Roosevelt's note seemingly claiming sole authorship until 1964. He realized that this note, together with the accounts of Rosenman and Burns of the writing of the address, had effectively removed him from what he considered his rightful place in the story of the creation of one of the most important speeches in American history.

Historians have not yet been quite able to settle the question. The most recent full-length account of the beginning of Roosevelt's Presidency, Frank Friedel's *Franklin D. Roosevelt: Launching the New Deal* (1973), in attempting to identify the author of the "nothing to fear" phrase, conflated Rosenman's and Moley's accounts into a rather odd, unsatisfying hybrid. However, the fact that no one has since added to the debate over the authorship of the first inaugural address suggests that there is probably a limit to how much historians care about the issue. The speech was Roosevelt's, no matter who wrote the words.

Inauguration day, March 4, 1933, was gray and cold, chilling the bodies and dimming the spirits of the people standing along Pennsylvania Avenue and gathered in front of the Capitol. Historians have tended to view this inauguration day weather as reflecting the hopelessness that had spread throughout the nation.

Roosevelt went to a brief church service before going to the White House to begin the inaugural events. He was apparently deeply moved by the trust that the American people had placed in him and he seemed himself to want to turn to someone beyond all of earth's troubles for help; he held his face in his hands for some moments, in private prayer.

Roosevelt arrived at the White House a little before 11 a.m.; he waited in the car while the President's party gathered in the White House. Finally, Hoover emerged and entered the open car, seating himself on Roosevelt's right. The Presidential cavalcade of seven cars began its brief journey up Pennsylvania Avenue to the Capitol. The President and the President-elect sat silently and awkwardly next to one another, the one a grim and frigid representative of the failed past, the other an ebullient and hopeful believer in a better future. The crowds cheered the two still figures in the open car, and finally Roosevelt began waving his hat in response. The two men said very little to one another; they never saw each other again after the inaugural ceremonies.

At the Capitol, Roosevelt had a few moments to look over his address. He wrote in a new opening line expressing the feeling of awe and reverence that had come over him that morning. "This is a day of national consecration," is the way he finally read the new line. At one o'clock the inaugural ceremonies began. Breaking with the custom of the new President saying simply "I do" after the Chief Justice's reading of the oath of office, Roosevelt repeated the entire oath. Then he turned to the waiting crowd and began his address.

The new President appeared grave; he did not smile once during the address. He spoke in a forceful and confident tone. It was time for the President to speak the truth, he said, and for the nation to face its problems honestly. He did not allow any doubt about the country's ability to solve its problems and to endure and prosper. "So, first of all, let me assert my firm belief," he called out to those gathered in front of him and to the many millions more across the nation listening to radios, "that the only thing we have to fear is fear itself — nameless, unreasoning, unjustified terror which paralyses needed efforts to convert retreat into advance."

He described the problems the nation faced: falling prices, rising taxes, shrinking personal and governmental income, a failure of the financial system, and, most important, unemployment. These were the country's "dark realities," which he blamed on the financiers who, through their incompetence, had brought on the ruin. He cast over these failed men the opprobrious biblical term "money changers." They were people moved by avarice; they had no vision. Americans would have to look elsewhere to find social values to which they could devote themselves.

Roosevelt made clear that he regarded the economic emergency as the equivalent of foreign invasion in its threat to the nation's existence. He outlined a program of drastic measures to meet the threat. His government would undertake great public works projects; would attempt to redistribute people away from the stricken industrial cities and back to the land, where they could find useful work; and would act to raise the values of agricultural products; to prevent foreclosures on homes and farms; to unify and thus improve the government's relief effort; to provide government supervision of the transportation, communications, and utilities industries, to strictly supervise banking and investment activities, and to provide an "adequate but sound currency," which did not by any means require a gold standard.

This was a drastic program for an American President to offer to the people. Certainly the nation has heard nothing like such a call for change in any inaugural address delivered since 1933. Roosevelt was aware that he was proposing a daring program, one that could only be realized by a President acting with the equivalent of wartime powers. If necessary, he felt, the Constitution could be stretched to allow the necessary executive action. He was determined to do what was required to put people back to work and repair the nation's institutional fabric. "I am prepared under my constitutional duty," he said, "to recommend the measures that a stricken Nation in the midst of a stricken world may require."

The President concluded his address by invoking traditional moral values of the American people and God's blessing. With this, after about 18 minutes of speaking, Roosevelt fell silent.

FDR delivers his first inaugural address at the Capitol, March 4, 1933. The day after the speech, President Roosevelt called Congress into a special session that lasted a "hundred days." Never before in the history of Congress had such far-reaching social and economic legislation been enacted in so short a time. (NPX-63-124, Franklin D. Roosevelt Library)

After listening to the speech with unusual quiet, the crowd of people who stood before him broke into loud approval. The millions at their radio sets in homes from end to end of the country must have felt a few goose bumps rise up on their skin. This certainly was something new — something hopeful. Although many of the conservatives who had been responsible for shaping the policies of the past decade were quick to attack and oppose the new President, most of the American people showed themselves willing to give him a chance. Many were enthusiastic supporters; many others were simply hopeful. Some wrote the President to tell him their feelings about the inaugural address. Most of the letters coming to the White House expressed favorable opinions. As one writer said, " It seemed to give the people, as well as myself, a new hold upon life."

Editorial opinion around the country was almost entirely favorable; even conservative newspapers joined in praise of Roosevelt's speech, which the *New York Herald Tribune* described as "A Call to Arms." The *Chicago Tribune* said that it struck "the dominant note of courageous confidence." The *Boston Transcript* felt that the "desperate temper of the people" required the kinds of drastic measures that the new President was prepared to undertake. The *Nashville Banner* said that Roosevelt was the great leader who had come forward to meet the demands of a troubled time. The *San Francisco Chronicle* wished the President well: "It is bold wisdom and action the people are praying for from President Roosevelt."

There were, of course, some who disagreed. Former President Hoover, to judge from the expressions which passed over his face as Roosevelt spoke, disagreed with practically everything the new President said. Outgoing Secretary of State Henry Stimson, who was later to be Roosevelt's Secretary of War, wrote in his diary that he was "thoroughly scared" by the inaugural address. "Like most of [Roosevelt's] past speeches," he wrote, "it was full of weasel words and would let him do about what he wanted to." An article in the *New Republic* expressed a similar fear. "The thing that emerges most clearly," it said, "is the warning of a dictatorship." Americans who agreed with such an opinion would probably have felt their fears deepening had they read the review of the new President's speech in the Italian fascist newspaper, *Il Giornale d'Italia*. "President Roosevelt's words," it said, "are clear and need no comment to make even the deaf hear that not only Europe but the whole world feels the need of executive authority capable of acting with full powers of cutting short the purposeless chatter of legislative assemblies."

Roosevelt's actions soon made clear that he was no dictator, but rather a President under the Constitution, chosen by the American people and expressive of their desire to solve their problems through the constitutional procedures that had served the country for 150 years. He was proof that America needed no dictator.

Within 48 hours of taking the oath of office, Roosevelt had signed a proclamation calling Congress into extraordinary session. What followed during the next 3 ½ months — the famous "Hundred Days" — was the passage of a remarkable body of legislation intended to prevent financial collapse and begin the difficult task of economic recovery. Many of the Roosevelt administration's alphabet agencies were born during this time — the CCC (Civilian Conservation Corps), AAA (Agricultural Adjustment Administration), TVA (Tennessee Valley Authority), and NRA (National Recovery Administration), for example.

By the end of this "Hundred Days" the work of recovery had been well begun. President Roosevelt would have two terms of office to bring the nation to a strength sufficient to meet the next great challenge to its survival — the Second World War.

The Facsimiles

Facsimile of the typed draft of President Roosevelt's first inaugural address, dated March 1, 1933, and delivered at the Capitol, March 4, 1933. The original typescript is in the Franklin D. Roosevelt Library, Hyde Park, NY.

Inaugural Address —

I am certain that my fellow Americans expect that

on my induction into the Presidency I will address them

with a candor and a decision which the present situation

of our nation impels.   This is preeminently the time

to speak the truth, the whole truth, frankly and boldly.

Nor need we shrink from ~~being~~ honest *by facing* as to the condition

of our country today.   This great nation will endure

as it has endured, will revive and will prosper.   So

first of all let me assert my firm belief that the only

thing we have to fear is fear itself, - nameless, unreasoning,

unjustified terror which paralyzes ~~the needed~~ *needed* efforts *To*

Convert retreat into advance.

~~to bring about prosperity once more.~~

~~In the crisis of our War for Independence; in the~~

~~poverty, the unrest and the doubts of the early days~~

~~of our constitutional government; later in the dark days~~

~~of the war between the states,~~ a leadership of frankness

and vigor met with that understanding and support of

the people themselves which is essential to victory.

I am convinced that you will again give that support to

leadership in these critical days.

In such a spirit on my part and on yours we (face)
our common difficulties. They are, thank God,
material things. Values have shrunken to
fantastic levels; taxes have risen ; our ability to
pay has fallen; government of all kinds is faced by
serious curtailment of income; the means of exchange
are frozen in the currents
of trade; industrial enterprise the withered leaves of lie in every wind; farmers
find no markets for their produce; the savings of many
years in thousands of families are gone.

More important, a host of unemployed citizens face
the grim problem of existence, and an equally great
number toil with little return. Only a foolish
optimist can deny the dark realities of the moment.

Yet our distress comes from no failure
of substance. We are stricken by no plague of locusts.
Compared with the perils which our forefathers conquered.

because they believed and were not afraid, we have

still much to be thankful for.   Nature still offers

her bounty and human efforts have multiplied it.

plenty *is at* our doorstep, but a vast use of it languishes

in the very sight of the supply.   Primarily, this is

because the rulers of the exchange of mankind's goods

have failed through their own stubbornness and their own

incompetence, have admitted their failure and abdicated.

Practices unscrupulous of the money changers stand indicted in the

court of public opinion, rejected by the hearts and

minds of men.

True, they have tried, but their efforts have been

cast ~~lost~~ in the pattern of an outworn tradition.   Faced

by failure of credit they have proposed only the lending

of more money.   Stripped of the lure of profit *by which* to

induce our people to follow their false leadership they

have resorted to exhortations, pleading tearfully for

restored confidence. ~~They~~ ~~They know~~ they

~~the~~ the ~~ancient~~ rules, *of a generation of self-seeking* They know ~~of no other ways~~ *only*

They have no vision, and when

there is no vision the people perish. ⁋ The money

changers have fled from their high seats in the temple

of our civilization.

We may now restore that temple to the ancient truths.

The measure of the restoration lies in the extent to

which we apply ~~standards of value~~ *social values* more ~~notably~~ noble

than mere monetary profit.

Happiness lies not in the mere possession of money;

it lies in the joy of achievement, in the thrill of

creative effort. The *joy and* moral stimulation of work must *no!*

be ~~no longer~~ *forgotten* ~~be~~ *themed* ~~in~~ *chase of* ~~the chase of~~ evanescent profits.

~~running.~~ These dark days will be worth all they cost

us if they *teach us that* ~~have led~~ ~~the truth~~ that our

true destiny is not to be ministered ~~to~~ unto but to

minister ~~not only~~ to ourselves and ~~but~~ to our fellowmen, ~~as well.~~

Recognition of the falsity of ~~money mere~~ material wealth standard of (~~real property~~) ~~success~~ goes hand in hand with the abandonment of the false belief that public office and high political position are to be valued only by the standards of pride of place and personal profit; There must be an end to a conduct in banking and in business which too often has given to a sacred trust the likeness of callous and selfish wrongdoing. Small wonder that confidence languishes, for it thrives only on honesty, on honor, on the sacredness of obligations, on faithful protection, on unselfish performance; ~~for~~ without them it cannot live.

Restoration calls, however, not for changes in ethics ~~government~~ alone This ~~The~~ nation asks for action, and action now.

Our greatest primary task is to put people to work.

This is no unsolvable problem if we face it wisely and

courageously.   It can be accomplished in part by direct

recruiting by the government itself, treating the task

as we would treat the emergency of a war, but at the same

time through this employment accomplishing greatly needed

projects to stimulate and reorganize the use of our natural

resources.

In ~~undertaking this work~~ *Hand in hand with this* we must ~~first~~ frankly

recognise the ~~past~~ overbalance of population in our industrial

centers and ~~endeavor~~ by engaging on a national scale in

a redistribution, *endeavor* to provide a better use of the land for

those best fitted for the land. ~~It~~ *The Task* can be helped by

definite efforts to raise the values of agricultural

products and with this the power to purchase the output of

our cities.   It can be helped by ~~treating~~ *by national* realistically the tragedy of the growing loss through foreclosure, of

our small homes and our farms.   It can be helped by insistence

that the federal, state and local governments act forthwith

on the demand that their cost be drastically reduced.   It

can be helped by the unifying of relief activities which today

are often scattered, ~~uneconomical~~ uneconomical and un

There are many ways in which ~~it can be helped~~, but

never ~~it~~ can ~~be~~ help ~~be~~ merely talking about it.   We must

act and act quickly.

~~So~~ ~~we can accomplish much~~ It can be helped by national planning

for and supervision of all forms of transportation and of

communications and other utilities which have a definitely

public character.

Finally, in our progress toward a resumption of work

we require two safeguards against a return of the evils of

the old order: there must be a strict supervision of all

banking and credits and investments; there must be an end

to speculation with other people's money, and there must be

provision for an adequate but sound currency.

These are the lines of attack.   I shall presently

urge upon a new Congress in special session detailed measures

for their fulfilment, and I shall seek the immediate

assistance of the several states.

Through this ~~joint~~ program of action we address ourselves

And making income beatimes

to putting our own national house in order.   Our international

trade relations though vastly important, are in point of

time and necessity secondary to the establishment of a sound

national economy.   I favor as a practical policy the putting

of first things first.   I shall spare no effort to restore

world trade by international economic readjustment, but the

emergency at home cannot wait on that accomplishment.

these

The basic thought that guides ~~the specific~~ specific

means of national recovery is not narrowly nationalistic.

~~It~~ .   It is *the* insistence, as a first consideration, upon the interdependence of the various elements in and

parts of the United States -- a recognition of the old and

permanently important manifestation of the American spirit of

the pioneer.   It is the way to recovery.   It is the immediate

way.   It is the strongest assurance that the recovery will

endure.

In the field of world policy I would dedicate this nation

to the policy of the good neighbor -- the neighbor who resolutely

respects himself and because he does so,respects the rights of

others -- the neighbor who respects his obligations and

respects the sanctity of his agreements in and with a world of

neighbors.

If I read the temper of our people correctly we now realize

as we have never realised before our interdependence on each

other: that we cannot merely take but we must give as well;

that we are to go forward we must ~~go forward~~ move as a trained and

loyal army willing to sacrifice ~~this thing or that thing~~ for the good of a~~the~~ common discipline, ~~and~~ Because without such

discipline no progress ~~can be~~ *is* made, ~~or any~~ *no* leadership ~~really~~

~~is.~~ *Effective* We are, I know, (ready and) willing to submit our

lives and property to such discipline because it makes

possible a leadership which aims ~~~~~~~~ at a larger good.

This I propose to offer ~~them~~, pledging ~~myself~~ that the

larger purposes will bind upon us all as a sacred obligation

with a unity of duty hitherto evoked only in time of armed

strife.

With *this* ~~my~~ pledge *Taken* ~~~~~, I assume unhesitatingly the ~~broad~~

~~~~ leadership of this great army of our people dedicated

to a disciplined attack upon our common problems.

Action in this image and to this end is feasible under

the form of government which we have inherited from our

ancestors.~~~~~ Our constitution is so simple and practical

that it is possible always to meet extraordinary needs by

changes in emphasis and arrangement without loss of

essential form. That is why our constitutional system

has proved itself the most superbly enduring political

mechanism the modern world has produced.   It has met every

stress of vast expansion of territory, of foreign wars, of

bitter internal strife, of world relations.

It is to be hoped that the normal balance of executive

and legislative authority may be wholly adequate to meet the

unprecedented task before us.   But it may be that an

unprecedented demand and need for undelayed action may call

for temporary departure from that normal balance of public

procedure.

I am prepared under my constitutional duty to ~~initiate~~ recommend

the measures that a stricken nation in the midst of a stricken

world may require.   These measures, or such other measures

as the Congress may build out of their experience and wisdom,

I shall, within my constitutional authority, ~~seek~~ to bring

to speedy adoption.

But in the event that the Congress shall fail to take

one of these two courses, and in the event that the national

emergency is still critical, I shall not evade the clear

course of duty ~~which~~ will then confront me.   I shall ask

the Congress for the one remaining instrument to meet the

~~course~~ -- broad executive power to wage a war against the

emergency, as great as the power that would be given to me

~~XXXX~~ if we were in fact invaded by a foreign foe.

For the trust reposed in me I will return the courage

and the devotion that befits the time.   I can do no less.

We face the arduous days that lie before us in the

warm courage of national unity; with the clear consciousness

of seeking old and precious moral values; with the clean

satisfaction that comes from the stern performance of duty

by old and young alike.   We aim at the assurance of a rounded

and permanent national life.

We do not distrust the future of essential democracy.

The people of the United States have not failed.   In their need they have registered a mandate that they want

direct vigorous action. They have asked for discipline

and direction under leadership.   They have made me the *present*

instrument, ~~the present humble instrument~~) of their

wishes.   In the spirit of the gift I take it.

In this dedication of a nation we humbly ask the

blessing of God. May he protect each and every one of

us. May he guide me in the days to come.

This was the final draft of the Inaugural at Hyde Park — Wed. March 1st 1933

Franklin D Roosevelt